All About Light

THIS EDITION
Editorial Management by Oriel Square
Produced for DK by WonderLab Group LLC
Jennifer Emmett, Erica Green, Kate Hale, *Founders*

Editors Grace Hill Smith, Libby Romero, Maya Myers, Michaela Weglinski;
Photography Editors Kelley Miller, Annette Kiesow, Nicole DiMella;
Managing Editor Rachel Houghton; **Designers** Project Design Company;
Researcher Michelle Harris; **Copy Editor** Lori Merritt; **Indexer** Connie Binder; **Proofreader** Larry Shec;
Reading Specialist Dr. Jennifer Albro; **Curriculum Specialist** Elaine Larson

Published in the United States by DK Publishing
1745 Broadway, 20th Floor, New York, NY 10019

Copyright © 2023 Dorling Kindersley Limited
DK, a Division of Penguin Random House LLC
23 24 25 26 10 9 8 7 6 5 4 3 2 1
001-333907-Oct/2023

All rights reserved.

Without limiting the rights under the copyright reserved above, no part of this publication may be reproduced, stored in or introduced into a retrieval system, or transmitted, in any form, or by any means (electronic, mechanical, photocopying, recording, or otherwise), without the prior written permission of the copyright owner.
Published in Great Britain by Dorling Kindersley Limited

A catalog record for this book
is available from the Library of Congress.
HC ISBN: 978-0-7440-7249-5
PB ISBN: 978-0-7440-7255-6

DK books are available at special discounts when purchased in bulk for sales promotions, premiums, fundraising, or educational use. For details, contact: DK Publishing Special Markets,
1745 Broadway, 20th Floor, New York, NY 10019
SpecialSales@dk.com

Printed and bound in China

The publisher would like to thank the following for their kind permission to reproduce their images:
a=above; c=center; b=below; l=left; r=right; t=top; b/g=background

123RF.com: Pornkamol Sirimongkolpanich / ,inlovepai 18br; **Dorling Kindersley:** NASA 10br; **Dreamstime.com:** Ulrich Allgaier 14-15, Narint Asawaphisith 20-21, Thanasak Boonchoong 16-17, Alexandre Dvihally 4br, Fedecandoniphoto 23clb, Fireflyphoto 1b, Markus Gann / Magann 6br, 23bl, gilmanshin 16br, 23tl, Cathy Keifer 21t, Andrey Kotko / Raccoonn 8-9, Sophy Kozlova 22clb, Lovelyday12 9t, Phillip Lowe 13b, Maximus117 19bl, 23cl, Mickem 15b, Nadezhda1906 12br, Nadind 5tc, Phittavas 21b, Photodynamx 3b, 12-13, Rina Selezneva 9bl, John Sirlin 18-19, Smileus 4clb, Snizhanna 4-5, Tom Wang 5c, 22br, Wenani 22, Nikolai Zotov 14br; **Getty Images:** Image Provided by Duane Walker 22cb; **Getty Images / iStock:** DonNichols 17b, E+ / photovideostock 11b, E+ / Pollyana Ventura 8br, Andrea Izzotti 5cra, republica 6-7; **Shutterstock.com:** Fer Gregory 20br, 23cla, Monkey Business Images 7b, Klagyivik Viktor 10-11

Cover images: *Front:* **Dreamstime.com:** Amelia Gama, Viktoriia Yatskina (BG);
Back: **Dreamstime.com:** Kdshutterman crb, Ykachan87 bl; **Shutterstock.com:** OsherR cla

All other images © Dorling Kindersley
For more information see: www.dkimages.com

For the curious
www.dk.com

Pre-level

All About Light

Ruth A. Musgrave

The world needs light. People and animals need light to see. Plants need light, too. Let's shine the light on light!

Let's begin with our biggest light. The Sun.

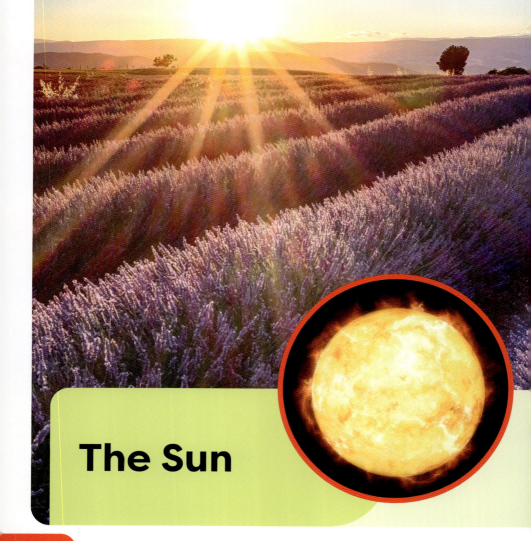

The Sun

The Sun shines on us.
The Sun lights
the world.

Sunlight warms the world. It helps plants grow, too.

sunlight

The Moon shines
in the night sky.
But it does not
make its own light.
Sunlight bounces
off the Moon.

Moon

Light looks white to us. But when it hits raindrops, it bends. Then, we see colors.

rainbow

Fire makes light.
Fire lights up
the night.

fire

People have learned how to make light. We use electricity.

How many lights do you see?

electricity

Flash! This is another kind of light.
It is made by electricity, too.
Light moves faster than sound.
That's why you see the flash.
Then, you hear it. **Boom!**

lightning

Some animals make light. Fireflies make light. They use it to talk to other fireflies in the dark.

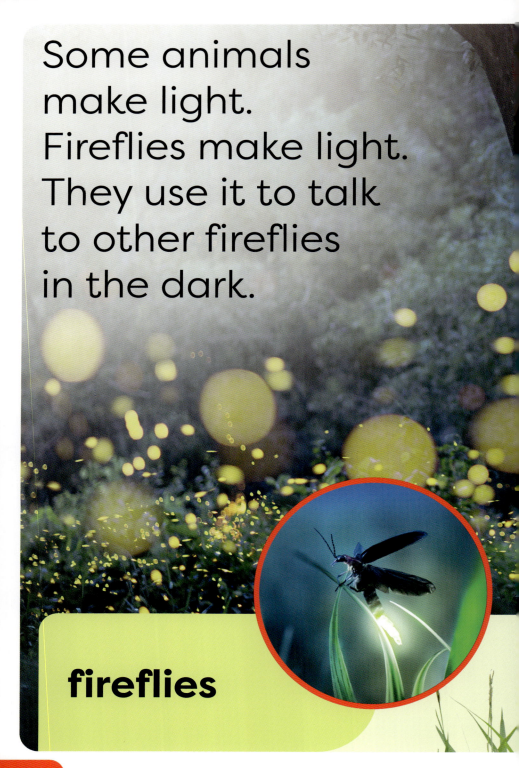

fireflies

The Sun makes light.
Fire and lightning make light.
Animals make light.
People make light.
Shine on, light!

Glossary

electricity
a kind of light

firefly
an insect that makes light

lightning
a kind of electrical energy

rainbow
created when light bends through raindrops

Sun
our biggest light

Quiz

Answer the questions to see what you have learned. Check your answers with an adult.

1. Name two things the Sun does.
2. What happens when light bends?
3. True or False: People have learned how to make light.
4. Why do you see lightning before you hear it?
5. How do fireflies use light?

1. The Sun lights and warms the world 2. It makes a rainbow
3. True 4. Light moves faster than sound
5. To talk to each other